The Giant in Kids

A Whole Child Development Guide

Mike R. Morrison

Table of Contents

Chapter 1

Amazing facts about Kids

I know you want the best for your kids!
But what if you're not receiving the truth about what genuinely is best?
Do you worry because your neighbor's kid is reading, while your little one isn't quite there yet?

Do you hear about all types of educational/athletic activities for tiny ones and feel that your kid may be missing out if they aren't exposed to enough of these structured programs?

Are you concerned you're not a good parent if you don't keep your kids occupied all the time?

If you responded yes to any of these questions, I'm not shocked. After all, there's no simpler group of people to terrify than parents!

There is a lot of misinformation out there! So, if you're bewildered and overwhelmed by the flood of parenting advice coming your way, you're not alone. How are you expected to filter through it all to determine what's actually best for your child?

Even when you feel you know what's best, you may be experiencing pressure from other sources! How do you reply when another parent shows disbelief that you haven't registered your kid in various programs? How can you stand up to the myths?

That's where I can assist!

I've come to grasp what small toddlers actually require. I know what the study tells us. And I know what child development demands. I'll break everything down for you – and help you feel more powerful as a parent. I can assist guarantee that your kid is happy and prospering.

You don't have to worry if your kid isn't reading as early as some other kids.

It's an acknowledged premise of motherhood that one of your major tasks is to educate your children - but it's never exactly apparent what you should put on the curriculum. However, I have learned more from my children than they have ever learned from me:

1. You have less authority than you imagine.

The amount of impact you have on children – or anybody else – is limited. Children, presumably the most pliable humans we come into intimate touch with, are yet totally their own people. Children are not simply miniature adults, but animals with a broad spectrum of diverse belief systems – and many of them are not subject to reason, argument, or anything else. They are enormously impressionable, it is true – but, critically, not in the manner you think or anticipate.

2. Selfishness, sloth, and egotism may be lovely.

No, I'm not talking about dads. I don't know how they get away with it, but kids are greatly inclined towards all of the above and still remain marvelous, attractive, and seductive. It's a trick some try to carry on into adult life. This tends not to work out nicely.

3. Rationality and fairness do not reign.

Children are likely to assume the erroneous notion that there is a right solution to all arguments – and that their parents would dutifully enforce it. Parents typically start out parenting thinking the same idea. However, it turns out that the way blame and punishment are assigned for any specifically claimed misdemeanor is as frequently as not decided by, at best, restricted facts and the bounds of adult reason; at worst by mendacity and low cunning, generally on the side of a sibling. Any given act is always unjust to someone. Parents find that, like governments, they have to make do with order rather than justice.

4. You are not as significant as you thought you were.

This typically comes as a particular shock to dads. Mothers figure it out the minute they are pregnant or long before. Fatherhood is essentially an exercise in achieving humility in the face of brutal circumstances. Until they have children, a lot of guys indulge in the illusion, consciously or not, that the world revolves around them. After children come, they recognize they have just made room for something far more essential than themselves - the next generation, which, at birth, is starting the urgent process of nudging their parents out of the way. Mothers tend to take this for granted. Fathers need to have it spelled out — again, and in some circumstances, endlessly.

5. Time goes quicker than you anticipated.

Once it passed at a sedate speed punctuated by the occasional wrinkle. Now you see it in continual quick motion as you observe the infinite changes in your children. Children educate you about ephemerality. And hence mortality.

6. Loving and liking are substantially unrelated.

If you haven't learned this previously through your spouse, your children are here to explain it to you.

7. Loving is better than being loved

You always believed you wanted someone to adore you. Then you learn that the great benefit of becoming a parent is not so much to be a target of someone else's affection but to have a repository for your own. To be liked is desired. To be able to love, it turns out, is necessary.

8. The world is more intricate than you anticipated.

Once upon a time, you assumed someone, somewhere had most of the answers even if you didn't. But confronted with the basic, continuous questioning of a toddler, you quickly learn that the universe largely includes unanswerable questions. How can you tell when sour cream goes bad? What color is a mirror? If a person is born deaf, what language do they think in?

It's not that these questions didn't exist previously. It's just that you didn't have to think about them. Now you realize how little you know. And, as Socrates' son or daughter probably painstakingly explained to him, it is the beginning of wisdom.

Chapter 2

Your Kids

Everyone is born with a specific personality type and distinctive attributes. Knowing your kid's temperament might help you understand why your child does the things they do. It may even assist you to address behavioral difficulties. Hippocrates classed people into four major kinds. Your kids may have qualities belonging to multiple groups. The strict categorization may not always be warranted. However, frequently, the kids may demonstrate the features of one certain personality type more vividly than others. The four personality types according to Hippocrates are:

Choleric

This personality type is passionate, assertive, competitive, determined, strong-willed, and adventurous.
Usually, choleric are goal-oriented and may be quite rational and analytical. They may not be extremely sociable.

Sanguine

This kind is bright, playful, inventive, chatty, and friendly.
Sanguine kids may be carefree, cheerful, adventurous, and not frightened of chances.
These kids could grow bored fast and have a hard time without amusement.

Melancholic

This personality type is profound, precise, polite, orderly, meticulous, and appreciative of traditions.
They are also sociable and want to be helpful.

These kids are not as fond of adventure or danger as other personality types.

Phlegmatic

This personality type is intelligent, attentive, controlled, and diplomatic. Kids with phlegmatic personality types frequently require intimate personal ties.
They are loyal, avoid confrontation, and like assisting others.

The four categories may potentially be simplified

1. Extraversion or introversion

This category defines a child's attention (inner or outward) (inner or outer). Extraverted children are extroverted and chatty, while introverts are quieter and self-reflective.

2. Sensing or intuition

This area has to do with how kids view the world around them.
Sensing folks are more prone to concentrate on reality and information at face value (what they can see and hear) (what they can see and hear).
Intuitive persons are more prone to see alternatives or hidden possibilities and prefer to concentrate more on the wider picture rather than precise details.

3. Thinking or feeling

Children in the thinking group are more factual and like to make judgments using logical reasoning.
Feeling persons are more inclined to be compassionate, understanding the effect of emotions on choices.

4. Judging or perceiving

Kids in the judgment group believe in rigid rules, order, and preparation. Perceiving kids enjoy a blank canvas, keeping their choices open for whichever route life takes them.
Personality is considered to continue to develop throughout numerous stages from birth through puberty. However, research has found three personality types that are expressed relatively early in life as soon as preschool age. These three categories continue throughout maturity. Besides, some suggest that these varied personality types contribute to diverse results in several areas, such as education, socializing, conduct and self-esteem.
The three personality types with their related qualities are:

1. Resilience

.Extraverted/Conscientious
.Good at regulating emotions
.Bounce back from adversity
.Self-confident
.Positive orientation toward others

2. Over controlled

.Shy
.Self-conscious
.Uncomfortable with strangers
.Low receptivity and readiness to try new things and helpful input from others
.Low flexibility
.Inhibited emotional expressiveness and poor emotional awareness.
.Low connectivity with others
Perfectionistic

3. Under controlled

.Disagreeable
.Lack self-control
.Low conscientiousness
.Low impulse control
.Emotionally dysregulated
.Aggressive

Just as no two kids are the same, no two parenting practices should be the same either. It's crucial to recognize children's personality types to know what they need to flourish. Sometimes, the temperaments of parents and their children appear to match well together. For some families, they are the cause of constant turmoil. It would surely be tough to have a very active kids living with relatively low-energy parents in a tiny apartment. However, it's vital to realize that kids can't alter their temperaments quickly. Knowledge of the components of your kid's personality, which are beyond their control, may lead you to a deeper understanding and acceptance of your child as they are.

Chapter 3

The indwelling Potentials

Every kid has his/her specific collection of potential. While some flourish academically, others select sports, arts, music, etc. to make the most of their talent. Children, from a very early age, start exhibiting indications of their potential in the form of interests, habits, and enthusiasm.

If parents keep a vigilant gaze they may immediately discover where the heart of their kids belongs to. The sooner parents recognize their kid's talents, the more time and opportunities their kids will obtain to grow their intrinsic abilities. To simplify matters and set the ball rolling for you, we have come up with the five easiest strategies to check your child's potential early.

Look for their interests

Children love to do so many things. From playing to painting, or reading to running, there is a range of things they prefer to perform throughout the day. And among them, there must be one object that will excite them the most. Since your kids spends the most time at home, figuring this out should not be a problem. For example, if your kids loves to draw, on paper, floor or walls, he/she may be interested in a creative sector like designing or architecture. Or if he/she loves to read, literature or writing might be on his/her mind.

Watch for their hobbies

Hobbies are separate from interests. They may be short-lived, like practicing guitar during summer vacation or rock climbing on a weekend adventure with the family. Your child's passion might be the place where his/her actual potential genuinely lies. Summer camps or weekend classes may be a superb technique to grow your child's enthusiasm and decide if he/she might build a career out of it. Talk to him/her about it to understand how far he/she is ready to take it. Do not be withdrawn from your kids on the issues of their interests. It may influence their professional path on a bigger scale.

Notice their passion for themes

Varied children have varied attitudes towards the stuff they study in school. Others enjoy math, others science, and some English. At home, they will study those things that they have formed a passion for. If you can't figure it out on your own, peek at your child's grades and they will reveal a lot about his/her excitement about the issue. If your child appreciates physics, then engineering or astrophysics may become his/her cup of tea when he/she grows up. Be there for them when they try to undertake experiments or practicals about that issue. They might blow up anything or not do it right, but if you don't back them, their mind won't proceed into inquiry to establish a suitable conclusion.

Never underestimate their enthusiasm for sports

There's more to potential than merely books and studies. Sports is one area in which kids are the most passionate. The sport your kids plays in his/her school and with friends can be where his/her talent sits. In today's day, when more children are taking up sports in school and turning it into a profession, athletics is one of the nicest jobs that one may pick. If your kids is interested in any sports, never hesitate to supply him/her with the competent guidance he/she needs to grow in it. If it needed you to take them there to the sports center yourself, do it. Give them morale-raising slogans like, "Go beat it", "You're a Champ", "Be the Best", etc.

Study their behavior

By behavior, we mean how people comport themselves in their friend groups, family circles, and social occasions. How people treat others and present themselves in the presence of others communicates a lot about their personality and interpersonal talents. Children who know how to tackle an issue all by themselves and have the ability to mix around do extraordinarily well in media, communication, marketing, sales, journalism, or management. If your child's interpersonal skills are greater than others and he/she loves to take the lead, he/she will do very well in one of these occupations.

As children develop and their abilities improve, their potential also expands with them. As teenagers grow more familiar with numerous topics, their interests develop and also alter with time. A nice home setting plays a very vital element in cultivating their potential to the greatest. The more support kids get from their parents to pursue a given field, the more focused and confident they feel in their skills. Make sure that as a parent you supply them with the help and guidance they need from you. Soon you will observe them develop and make the most of their potential.

Raising children is a major task in today's climate. Peers and pop culture exert a never-ending strain on kids. Parents usually feel helpless, as every godly notion, they teach their children seems to be challenged by the corrupt ideals of this imperfect world. But the good news is, that God has a plan for effectively raising your children and you can learn from it. Follow these steps and you'll transition from struggling parents to one with a vision for their children's future and a bright one at that.

Chapter 4

Raising Champs

It's good to have winners and losers. Not keeping score is a useless effort to coddle our children and keep them protected in a bubble. This will end up backfiring as we produce an epidemic of entitled kids whose self-esteem has been constructed on a house of cards. Kids need to learn how to win graciously and lose gracefully. As someone much wiser than me has stated, "We need to prepare our children for the road, not construct the route for our children." But just because you keep score, doesn't mean you have to stress victory. They are not the same thing. As adults, we need to praise and reward the process, not the end. Praise the effort, not the score. Praise the progress, not the win/loss record.

At the young level, anything that is done to maximize the possibility of winning diminishes the overall growth and pleasure of the game for the kids engaged.

When you emphasize winning, you create an atmosphere where your kids dread making errors. But errors are the essential component of growth and development!
You reward the more mature and advanced kids and leave the rest behind. You educate your kids that the result is more important than the method. That is a very hazardous mindset to foster if your objective is to create happy and successful children.

I want to politely address parents that yell directions to their kids from the sideline. While I know this is well meant, it hinders growth and makes the game a lot less entertaining for the kids. As parents, we should be applauding, encouraging, and supporting our little rascals, and expressing praise when appropriate. Screaming 'shoot' or 'pass' at the top of your lungs does not add value nor does it assist. In reality, it increases pressure, and uncertainty, and robs the kids of probably the most critical skill set in athletics - the capacity to make judgments. From a basic viewpoint, shooting the ball should be an activity, not a response! Lastly, it weakens the coach.

Our kids should only get direction from one person during competition — their coach.

As parents and coaches, we should all be promoting enjoyment and growth and recognizing strong attitudes and work ethics, not berating referees, crowning National Champions, and fostering a win-at-all-costs, high-pressure atmosphere. So, how can we do that? What are some pointers to doing kid's sports right? Research has found that the best 3 sentences you can say to your kid after a practice or game are:

I love to watch you play.
How easy is that?
I love to see you get out there and be yourself!

That's it.!
Give them a hearty embrace!

That comment has been a game changer for me (pun intended) (pun intended). I have conditioned myself to say that to my kids every time. And without fail, their faces light up with a wide grin when I do. Please try it.

Another option is for you to provide your kids with these 4 reminders before every practice and every game:

.Have fun
.Play hard
.Listen to your coach
.Be a good teammate

If they can perform those 4 things every time they enter the court or field, then kids will be enjoying the full advantage that sports give at such an impressionable age. I also want to propose you encourage your children to continue active in as many sports as they can for as long as they can. Both individual sports like golf, tennis, and martial arts, and team sports like basketball, baseball, and soccer, is beneficial for them psychologically and physically. It will allow them time to determine what they are excellent at and what they are most enthusiastic about.

Early sport specialization is the incorrect choice. Trust me. Encouraging your children to play numerous sports in elementary and middle school will in no way hinder their possibility for future success in one specific sport. Believing that a kid has to play one sport, only one sport, year-round starting at age 8 or 9, is a hazardous trend that is entirely incorrect. Playing several sports throughout the year provides many advantages. The biggest one is it helps minimize burnout and overuse problems.

This tendency started when parents (unintentionally) began bastardizing the '10,000 Rule' by Malcolm Gladwell (which asserts it takes around 10,000 hours of dedicated effort to perfect a skill) (which states it takes approximately 10,000 hours of deliberate practice to master a skill). This contains two blatant mistakes. One, the research he linked was with musicians (pianists), not athletes. There is a tremendous contrast in the physical toll imposed on a child's body between practicing the piano and playing competitive basketball (for example) (for example). And two, the key is DELIBERATE practice.

"Deliberate practice refers to a unique sort of practice that is deliberate and methodical. While ordinary practice could contain thoughtless repetitions, purposeful practice demands concentrated attention and is undertaken with the sole objective of increasing performance." — James Clear

So merely having a kids 'play 10,000 hours of basketball from age 8 to 18' is NOT what Gladwell meant. Logging hours is not the solution. All training has to be intentional, purposeful, and deliberate. Having been engaged in top basketball my whole life - I can assure you that 95% of what is now going on during kid's practices and training sessions is not purposeful practice.

On a separate, but equally essential matter, the notion of 'everyone-gets-a-trophy' to enhance children's self-esteem does not work. It promotes a false feeling of success, and entitlement, and fosters fragile egos.

By definition, it's not an achievement until it is earned.

Personally, as a parent, I do not allow my children beat me in any sports of talent, strength, or speed. No, I am not a sociopath. I do this to educate children about life. When I win, I teach them the significance of losing with elegance and grace. In games of talent, strength, or speed, I will frequently handicap the rules (EX: giving them a huge head start in a race) to give them greater odds. However, I still try my hardest to defeat them. In many circumstances, with the correct handicap, they will win. When they do, I praise them and tell them how pleased I am with their effort, I appreciate how hard they worked, how much they practiced, and how they never stopped. I take care to recognize the process, not the result. I don't make a big deal when they win/lose, but rather stress the impact their work and attitude had.

Most importantly, I always demonstrate the right conduct whether I win or lose. I am convinced that my position will educate my children to appreciate the process, embrace the practice, always make a tremendous effort, earn everything in their lives, and manage both winning and losing with class.

And THAT is the secret to being happy, satisfied, and successful!

Let's work together to maintain the purity of youth sports and raise our kids to bring true contributions to the world.

Chapter 5

"Twinkle Twinkle Little Stars"

These words from the classic 19th Century poetry, penned by Jane Taylor, center on the dignity of a light blazing brilliantly, something we don't entirely grasp but that is also useful along our route. It's dazzling and it's free.

Today, we sing songs to feel good and to appreciate their melodies as much as their content and context. In the end, they will survive for many more years and bring many more smiles and many more interpretations as time goes.

In resemblance to kids, when everything and everything is dark, their brilliance shines. Their brightness brightens the darkness. They become the reason why you as a parent go out to work. The reason why you're accountable and the reason in most circumstances, why you're giving life attempts and opportunities. They are extremely important to how you shape your schedule and how you arrange your day. Never will you be exhausted in caring and addressing their vital calls. Don't ever give them the idea that you're getting alienated from them. Thats why you have to allow that link and friendship with your kids blossom from when they're tiny. They require reproof when you suspect they're shifting to a specific lane that may damage their future.

For everything you do as a parents, don't cease reigniting the spark in children. You're the sun, they are the stars. Your words, attitudes, lives and motherhood should always reflect some light in them. The reason for this is, whatever job route they take, that light will stay.

When I led the way for my kids to give offering in Church, I didn't realize it would have big consequences on them. As time rolls by, those young folks began departing the chairs before me. I also discovered that they are not afraid to hand away some money. When I give them anything, I encourage them to share with Friends. I subsequently learned that I don't need to remind them anymore. They've carried the light that mysteriously came from me. When I read, I invite them to join me. Most times, they look through picture books and sketch. When it became part of them, I recognized that they've subconsciously included it to their daily agenda. They learn them subconsciously and take up those light. Try not to lead darkness as parents.

Your children are continuously monitoring what you do. They notice how you manage stress. They monitor how you treat other people and notice how you cope with your emotions. They absorb up all that knowledge like tiny sponges. Even when you believe your children aren't paying attention, it's crucial to be a good role model.

According to the social learning hypothesis, individuals learn by observing others.
For instance, the classic Bobo doll experiment illustrated how kids copy adult behavior. Researchers observed that kids handled a doll the same way the adults did.

Children who witnessed an adult become hostile with the doll were aggressive in their relationships as well. Meanwhile, kids who witnessed adults treat the doll warmly mimicked the generosity.

You probably don't need a sophisticated scientific experiment to observe that kids copy their parents. You undoubtedly notice it every day.

When you're sweeping the floor, you could see your little one pretending to sweep too. Or, you could hear your preschooler put her plush bear to bed the same way you tuck her up at night. Kids repeat what they hear, and they copy what they see. For this reason, you need to be careful of the things you're unknowingly teaching your kid.

What Behavior Are You Modeling?

Sometimes, you could unwittingly imitate harmful habits for your kids. Consider these possibilities.

A lady tells the cashier at a restaurant that her 12-year-old kid is only 11, so she may receive a discount at the buffet. Her son learns cheating. Trust me. He learns lying gradually. Her kid learns it's OK to lie occasionally to achieve what you want.
A father spends his nights watching television, but tells his 14-year-old daughter she should read more.
Parents teach their kids to treat everyone with respect. Yet, they regularly make negative remarks about other individuals behind their backs.
A divorced couple disputes constantly over custody problems and visits, yet they want their kids to get along with one another.
A mom advises her kid to stop putting his fingers in his mouth; however when she's frightened, she chews her fingernails.
A mother encourages her daughter to be polite to others, yet she shouts at the shop clerk when the business refuses to accept back an item she wishes to return.
A father tells his kids that they should eat properly, but he steals dessert after they go to bed.
Parents teach their kids to share and be kind with what they have, but they never make donations or become engaged in any form of charity or volunteer activity.
A father smokes cigarettes. While he holds a cigarette in his hand, he warns his kids that smoking is bad and that they should never take up the habit.
Parents urge their kids to accept responsibility for their actions and their decisions. Yet, when parents forget about their child's dental appointment, they quarrel with the receptionist and tell her she certainly made a scheduling mistake.

According to the social learning hypothesis, individuals learn by observing others.
For instance, the classic Bobo doll experiment illustrated how kids copy adult behavior. Researchers observed that kids handled a doll the same way the adults did.

Children who witnessed an adult become hostile with the doll were aggressive in their relationships as well. Meanwhile, kids who witnessed adults treat the doll warmly mimicked the generosity.

You probably don't need a sophisticated scientific experiment to observe that kids copy their parents. You undoubtedly notice it every day.

When you're sweeping the floor, you could see your little one pretending to sweep too. Or, you could hear your preschooler put her plush bear to bed the same way you tuck her up at night. Kids repeat what they hear, and they copy what they see. For this reason, you need to be careful of the things you're unknowingly teaching your kid.

Follow Your Own Rules

It's incredibly hard to model acceptable conduct for your kids all the time, and no one is expecting you to be flawless. But you should endeavor to model the rules and habits you want your kids to follow.

If you want your kids to be true, you should aim to be honest. For example, if you utter white lies rather than being honest, your kids will learn that lying is okay.

Show your kids how to obey your family rules by demonstrating them every time you have.

Likewise, apply punishment that teaches life skills, and explain how these rules will aid them later in life. If you demonstrate kids that you obey the rules, it will boost the efficacy of your disciplinary tactics.

There may be situations when you need to clarify any judgments that can be perplexing.

For instance, if your buddy bakes you a cake, and you think it tastes bad, you still may tell them it was excellent to spare their emotions. When anything like that occurs, you'll want to explain to your children that you didn't want to harm your friend's emotions.

Model Life Skills

You also have opportunity every day to live a life worth imitating. Think about what you want your kids to learn from you and strive to replicate it in your life. Naturally, there may be occasions when you make errors or don't accomplish things precisely as you had intended. But, that is OK.

When that occurs, use the opportunity to speak to your kids about where you fell up and how you want to be better next time.
Kids learn essential things from you even when you make errors.

For instance, if you handle bad mistakes with grace and don't beat yourself up, they'll also learn to be nice to themselves when they mess up. Here are some examples of additional things you can model for your kids. Use these suggestions to become a good role model, or come up with ideas of your own.

Live a Healthy Life

When you eat properly and exercise on a regular basis, you're setting a positive example for your kids. Plus, if you are making nutritious meals and eliminating fast food, you are helping your kids prevent childhood obesity.

Of course, try not to be pushy or restricting in your attempts to set a good example. Being controlling about food or stressing about how your body (or your child's body) appears, might lead to body image difficulties and eating disorders.

Show Respect and Teach Empathy

Every parent wants to raise kids who are nice to others. This aim becomes a reality when you exhibit respect and empathy in your own life. Be courteous to everyone you contact with and soon your kids will be doing the same.

Whether it's the cashier at the grocery store or the waiter in your favorite restaurant, smile, say please, and thank you, and before long your kids will be doing it too.

Allow your kids to witness you being compassionate and attentive to others too. Use scenarios that occur around you to speak about how others may be experiencing. Teaching kids to be empathic is one of the greatest methods to prevent them from bullying others.

Tackle Technology Issues

If you are like most parents, you worry about the amount of screen time your kids are receiving each day. Whether it is the time younger children spend watching programs and playing online games, or it is the time adolescents spend on social media, every parent fears that their kids are in front of a screen too regularly.

But before you can say anything to your kids, take a look at the amount of time you're spending in front of a device.

Even if you're working, answering emails, and doing activities you deem constructive, you are still setting an example for your kids. Address your technology usage first, and then try to create some guidelines for the kids.

Work Hard

Developing a solid work ethic is a life skill every kid needs. Whether it is working hard in school, at a part-time job, or on a sports team, kids need to have a good work ethic. The greatest method to inculcate this ability is to first model it at home.

Whether you go to work every day or you work from home, let your kids to see you working. Even completing chores together as a family is a terrific approach to build a healthy work ethic in your kids.

Volunteer in the Community

When you volunteer in the community, you're telling your kids that you care about the world they live in.
And, kids learn to care too. Whether you volunteer in the schools, engage in a neighborhood clean-up initiative, or give food and supplies to the local food bank, you're telling your kids what goes on outside of your house is important—that giving back is critical to make the world a better place.

You also may get your kids engaged in volunteering. When they frequently serve others, even if it is in a modest manner, they will learn to appreciate what they have.

Demonstrate Social and Emotional Skills

Pay attention to emotional and social skills too.

Show your children how to greet someone and how to ask questions when they are confused. Instruct them on how to meet new friends and invite others to join in. Demonstrate how to manage emotions, like frustration or sadness. Talk about your emotions when you are unhappy, angry, or sad, and urge others to do the same.

Prevent Behavior Problems by Teaching Your Child About Feelings

Teach New Skills

When you want to teach your children anything new, whether it's how to make their bed or how to tie their shoes, show them how you do it. Then, let them practice it on their own. Showing, rather than telling, might be the greatest approach for kids to acquire a number of new abilities

Chapter 6

The Giants in Kids

Your main role as a parent is to help shape your kids into nice, respectable, honest, and loving persons. And, sometimes the best way to achieve it is to be a good role model. This may entail taking a deeper look at your behaviors and making some adjustments. But, if you do, both you and your kids will profit.

There's a fire that resides inside every kids. It simply has to be lighted, then you'll witness a wild flaming forest. It's your obligation as a parent to make sure that the fire doesn't go adversely crazy but in a good way. It's on your watch and direction that your kids won't grow trolls as giants but BFG (Big Friendly Giant).

You nourish them. You guide them. You encourage them. You advise them. You reproof them when required. You make them accept responsibility. All these and more are methods you build the positive giants in your kids.

When I was small, I pretty don't know much about subjects. I could hardly read. I was terrified about going to school. I avoided such socialization since I couldn't handle the environment of learning and being punished. Then my Mum got involved. She began giving me home lessons at night and made sure I read daily. Within a short amount of time, I recognized that I've gone steps above my dullness. I was growing sharper. I was reading fluently and I couldn't believe it. Gradually, I soared extremely well in academic tasks and I became a top kids. Winning accolades and receiving plaudits. One element that fashioned my work is the mentoring of my Mum. She did more to explain figures, alphabets, and words to me. That fire never went cold again. It flared brighter in me.

You must have the narrative of Ben Carson(MD). From being a dullard in class to a champion. At 33, he was the youngest Chief of Pediatrics

Neurosurgery in the United States. Also became the first Neurosurgeon to separate conjoined twins together with his team.
It wasn't all green growing up for him, but his mother had a vital part in his life and destiny. Don't ever ignore your kids. Watch them like the mother hen. Be the reason they wake up with fresh hope and inspiration daily.

Most renowned individuals you know today also had an excellent parental foundation to release that fire in them.

You're not alone when you feel that bringing up your kid is a wonderful yet stressful endeavor. Every parent would confess that seeing their young ones grow up is a fascinating adventure, particularly when you have someone else as competent supporting you. For many, that someone is a facility that provides the finest daycare in Sydney.

Other than their physical growth and development, you also need to teach vital values to your kid to assist them to become better individuals in the future. It may seem so large today, but there are stages.
Let's review some of the strategies which parents have utilized to effectively raise children who are disciplined, talented, well-behaved, and capable of accomplishing tremendous accomplishments. They include:

1. Feed Their Curiosity

Your child's interest surges when they start questioning and engaging with their environment throughout their early years. Their curiosity encourages children to examine objects and people around them which then provides a channel to train their brains as they learn to comprehend. It is at this time when your kid finds their hobbies or you may notice what catches their attention more.

To help them uncover their entire potential, engage them by replying to their numerous inquiries regardless of how superficial they may appear. You may also listen to their tales as muddled up as they may seem since this expands their brain capabilities. By stimulating your child's curiosity, you can assist them to uncover their interests which you may subsequently cultivate into skills.

2. Do Not Dictate Their Likes

It is tempting to keep steering your child's choices to what you believe is best for them, right? That is true for a majority of parents also. However, before you force your kid toward things you enjoy or have picked for them, you should take a step back and examine whether they genuinely appreciate your taste. Even if you are responsible for your baby's existence, enabling them to explore other channels may bring up skills you wouldn't have anticipated.

You can be enjoying reading for pleasure and want your kid to follow your path. While reading is beneficial for them, you may be locking the world's next famous chef up in a pastime they'll never warm up to. To prevent this, let your kid try out things on their own and you just may be astonished at what they are capable of

3. Practice Patience

It isn't easy for any parent who's spent a full day at work to stay up late and listen to their kid speak about everything and nothing at all. Your kids can want you to observe while they produce a paper art or model a clay figure even though you have plenty on your plate. While minor efforts like these by your kid may seem unimportant, your presence and support feed their passion and this can turn out to be their job later in life.

Most prominent artists all over the globe are known to owe their initial steps to childhood discoveries. Even if your child's hobbies may not always come within your area of interest, you should be patient and provide assistance to allow them to find who they truly want to be.

4. Accommodate Mistakes

Remember how it felt when your employer or partner scolded you for a mistake you had no control over? Now imagine this impact on your kid after you chastise them for indulging in things they regard to be pleasurable. Since your kid is in their exploration period, they are going to get into trouble as they test out items around them. While scolding them makes them more attentive next time, you should let some little errors pass.

Breathing down your child's neck or criticizing all their movements diminishes their potential. This is because your kids develops a phobia of testing their ideas out and instead recedes to a corner without incentive to explore.
Shouting at them over split paints, filthy clothing, and painted skin are among things that will discourage your child's desires and vice versa.

For a skill or ability to completely develop itself, there is a range of external and contextual elements. How much time and energy does your kid spend practicing, acquiring, or studying a specific skill? Do financial, economic, and societal variables impact your child's capacity to develop their talent? What can you do as a parent to assist and nurture the development of your child?

1. Identify
After your children's classes cease or the season ends, work with them to identify an area that speaks to them, one they are excellent at. Sometimes, kids need to attempt several various classes before arriving at the perfect

sport, musical instrument, hobby, or academic career. Mark your kids when they are engaging in an activity.

2. Let them Fly
In the process of aiding them, DO NOT push your childhood goals to become the purpose of their sensitive, young days, Raising kids with character means enabling them to go through their unique obstacles and develop into their strengths. The responsibility of the parent is to establish a safe atmosphere for them to stumble, fall, get back up, dust themselves off, receive a hug and a confidence booster, and try again until they can fly. At that time, they'll have the life lessons and essential skills to go at it on their own, and voilà! They'll be off and running, realizing their potential. Let them cruise about on their routes, discover their new methods, and so, declare to the great world 'what they have.

Just be there to Guide and steer them. Reproof when required.

www.ingramcontent.com/pod-product-compliance
Lightning Source LLC
LaVergne TN
LVHW020542160826
845677LV00015B/4159